Do NOT say "fart!"

Written and Illustrated by
Jennifer Price Davis

Dedication

To my kid, with all the love in the world.

Hey there!
Just a friendly reminder.

Do NOT say "f---!"

You know... That word that starts with a rumble in your belly.

Did you know it actually starts in your large intestine?

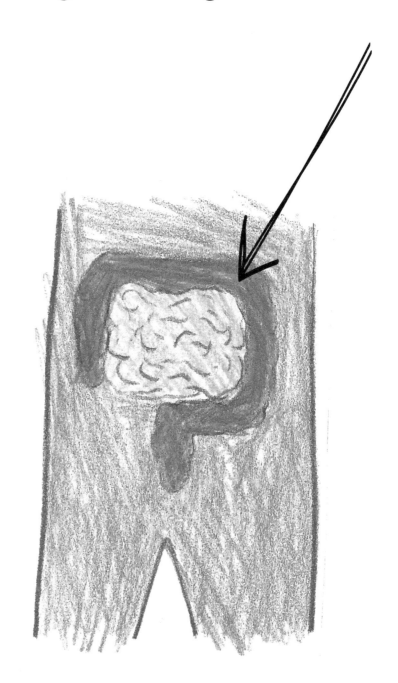

Then it travels down, down, down, and out through your...

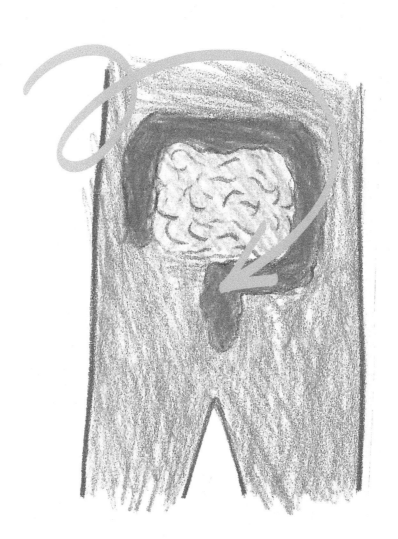

Don't say "butt" either!

It's not really a bad word. It's just that some people think it's not polite to say "fa--!"

Instead, you can say:

"Toot,"

"poot,"

or "break wind."

That one sounds like a science experiment.

"Pass gas" is a good one.

There is also, "rip one."
Ew!

"Cut the cheese" is a popular one.

Now I'm hungry!

Last but not least,
you can say, "flatulence"

if you're fancy.

But whatever you do,

do not say,

"FAR-!"

Phew! That was close!!

Now, if you toot, poot, break wind, rip one, cut the cheese, or have flatulence... Do say "Excuse me."

But whatever you do, do not say

FART!

Oops!

Excuse me.

About the Author

Hello! I'm Jennifer Price Davis. I'm an artist, living and working in Cleveland, Ohio. I love using art and words to create worlds, smiles, and giggles!

I've illustrated and written many children's books, and I've painted more pictures than I can count. I love making art. I believe we are all creative and magical in our own way. When we share our magic, we make the world a much better and brighter place.

I hope you share your magic with the world!

Thank you for reading my book.

To see more art and books, you can visit my website, www.jenniferpricedavis.com!